CULTURE IN ACTION

Art For All

Public Art

Laura J. Hensley

Raintree

Chicago, Illinois

www.heinemannraintree.com
Visit our website to find out more information about Heinemann-Raintree books.

To order:

☎ Phone 888-454-2279

🖳 Visit www.heinemannraintree.com to browse our catalog and order online.

©2011 Raintree
an imprint of Capstone Global Library, LLC
Chicago, Illinois

Edited by Louise Galpine, Megan Cotugno, and Abby Colich
Designed by Ryan Frieson
Original illustrations ©Capstone Global Library, Ltd.
Illustrated by Cavedweller Studio, Randy Schirz
Picture research by Liz Alexander
Originated by Capstone Global Library, Ltd.
Printed and bound in China by China Translation & Printing Services, Ltd.

14 13 12 11 10
10 9 8 7 6 5 4 3 2 1

Library of Congress Cataloging-in-Publication Data
Hensley, Laura.
  Art for all : what is public art? / Laura Hensley.
      p. cm. -- (Culture in action)
  Includes bibliographical references and index.
  ISBN 978-1-4109-3923-4 (hc)
  1. Public art--Juvenile literature. I. Title.
  N8825.H46 2010
  701'.1--dc22
                                2009051126

Acknowledgments

The author and publishers are grateful to the following for permission to reproduce copyright material:

We would like to thank the following for permission to reproduce photographs: © 2010 Banco de México Diego Rivera Frida Kahlo Museums Trust, Mexico, D.F. / DACS p. **21** (Alamy/Photos 12); © ARS, NY and DACS, London 2010 p. **18** (Getty Images/Hulton Archive); © Chris How p. **25**; © Estate of Robert Smithson/DACS, London/VAGA, New York 2010 p. **24** (Corbis/George Steinmetz); Alamy pp. **7** (© Kokyat Choong), **27** (© Simon Hadley); Corbis pp. **10** (© Werner Forman), **14** (© Guo Jian She/Redlink); Shutterstock pp. **4** (© PixAchi), **6** (© Julie Lucht), **8** (© Vinicius Tupinamba), **11** (© Jeff Banke), **12** (© Bartlomiej Magierowski), **15** (© Kharidehal Abhirama Ashwin), **16** (© Bryan Busovicki), **17** (© ostill), **19** (© Terry Walsh), **22** (© Glenn Walker), **26** (© Kevin Connors).

Cover photograph of Jeff Koons's living statue of a flower-covered puppy at the Guggenheim Museum in Bilbao, Spain reproduced with permission of Alamy (© Danita Delimont).

We would like to thank Susie Hodge and Jackie Murphy for thier invaluable help in the preparation of this book.

Every effort has been made to contact copyright holders of any material reproduced in this book. Any omissions will be rectified in subsequent printings if notice is given to the publisher.

All the Internet addresses (URLs) given in this book were valid at the time of going to press. However, due to the dynamic nature of the Internet, some addresses may have changed, or sites may have changed or ceased to exist since publication. While the author and Publishers regret any inconvenience this may cause readers, no responsibility for any such changes can be accepted by either the author or the Publishers.

Author

Laura J. Hensley is an editor and writer who specializes in topics related to art and literature.

Literacy consultant

Jackie Murphy is Director of Arts at the Center of Teaching and Learning, Northeastern Illinois University. She works with teachers, artists, and school leaders internationally.

Expert

Susie Hodge is an author and artist with nearly 60 books in print. She has an MA in the History of Art from the University of London and is a Fellow of the Royal Society of Arts. She teaches and lectures on practical art and art and design history to students of all ages.

Contents

Some words are printed in bold, **like this**. You can find out what they mean by looking in the glossary on page 30.

Art All Around You

You probably walk past a work of art every day. Perhaps there is a **memorial**, such as a sculpture honoring local soldiers. Or maybe there is a statue of an important person, or **murals** painted on the sides of buildings? What about posters?

All these kinds of art, and more, are public art. They are works of art that are created to be displayed in a public place, where everybody can experience them.

Making public art

Different people and groups pay for public art. This can affect the final work of art. For example, sometimes a government pays for public art. This government might want the art to present a certain image—perhaps a statue that makes a leader seem brave and strong.

U.S. artist Jeff Koons's Puppy (1992) is made from thousands of flowers.

But sometimes artists are allowed to choose what they want to express. They can use public art to make people feel emotions or think about ideas.

Experiencing public art

Public art is all around you! **Political** (government-related) art can create a sense of national pride. Religious art might inspire people, while memorials can cause them to **reflect** (think closely). **Abstract** or lighthearted works of art allow people to appreciate beauty or have a laugh.

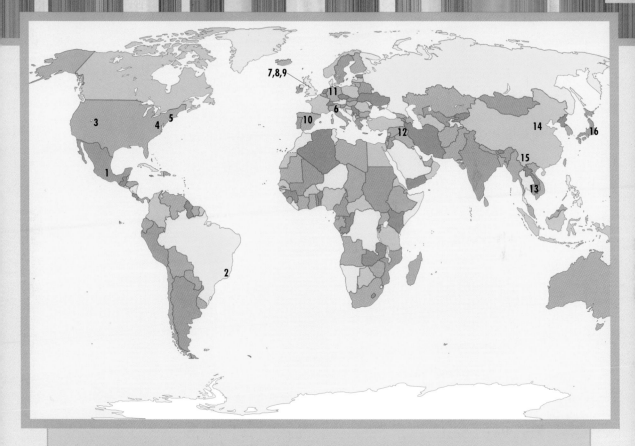

Use this map to see where the works of public art mentioned in this book were made.

1. Mexico City, Mexico:
Diego Rivera's murals on government buildings (page 21)

2. Rio de Janeiro, Brazil:
Paul Landowski's *Christ the Redeemer* (page 17)

3. Salt Lake City, Utah:
Robert Smithson's *Spiral Jetty* (page 24)

4. Washington, D.C.:
Maya Lin's Vietnam Veterans Memorial (page 7)
Lincoln Monument (page 6),
Washington Monument (page 11)

5. New York City:
Richard Serra's *Tilted Arc** (page 18),
Christo and Jean-Claude's *The Gates** (page 26)

6. Rome, Italy:
Arch of Constantine (page 11)
Michelangelo's *Pietà* (page 16)

7. London, England:
Victoria and Albert Memorial (page 6)
Nelson's Column (page 11)
Antony Gormley's *One & Other** (page 27)

8. Gateshead, England:
Antony Gormley's *Angel of the North* (page 19)

9. West Sussex, England:
Andy Goldsworthy's *Chalk Stone Trails* (page 25)

10. Bilbao, Spain:
Jeff Koons's *Puppy* (cover, page 4)

11. Berlin, Germany:
Peter Eisenman's Holocaust Memorial (page 8)

12. Northern Iraq:
Black Obelisk of Shalmaneser III (page 10)

13. Cambodia:
Angor Wat (page 15)

14. Luoyang, China:
Longmen Caves (page 14)

15. Lijiang, Yunnan, China:
Mao Zedong statue (page 12)

16. Tokyo, Japan:
Sogetsu Ikebana flower show (page 25)

*no longer in place

Memorials

Memorials are a popular form of public art. These works of art honor the lives of others. Memorials are also sometimes called **monuments**.

War memorials

Governments often **commission**, or request and pay for, memorials honoring people who have served their countries. Throughout history, war memorials had a typical style. They usually featured sculptures of **heroic** (brave) servicemen and servicewomen.

This statue honors a British war veteran.

Remembering past leaders

Throughout the world, memorials and monuments honor great people from a country's past. For example, the Albert Memorial (1876) in London, England, honors Prince Albert, the husband of Queen Victoria. The Lincoln Monument (1922) in Washington, D.C., honors President Abraham Lincoln. Such works are usually commissioned by a government and placed in important public areas.

A new kind of memorial

In 1982 U.S. student Maya Lin created a different kind of memorial. The U.S. hosted a design competition to create a memorial in Washington, D.C., to honor the U.S. soldiers who died in the Vietnam War (1954–75).

Lin designed two black granite walls, arranged in a V-shape. The names of dead and missing soldiers were carved into these walls. By listing every name, Lin's memorial honors each person individually. Seeing the nearly 60,000 names also makes visitors **reflect** on how many lives were lost.

Controversy

Some people were upset because they felt the memorial was not clearly understandable. So the U.S. government commissioned a more traditional work by sculptor Frederick Hart to be placed nearby. This sculpture (1984) shows three heroic-looking soldiers.

Which style of memorial do you think is more effective? Why?

Lin's Vietnam Veterans Memorial (1982) is now widely admired.

Holocaust memorials

For years, people have struggled with ways to remember the **Holocaust**. This was when eleven million people, including six million European Jews, were killed from 1933 to 1945, under Adolf Hitler's Nazi government.

The Berlin Holocaust Memorial

Over 50 years after the Holocaust, the German government chose U.S. **architect** Peter Eisenman to create a Holocaust memorial in the center of Berlin, the capital city.

Eisenman's Holocaust Memorial is made up of 2,711 concrete slabs arranged in a large grid. There are no images of people and no words or names. Eisenman meant for visitors to wander through the slabs and feel lost, even scared—like the victims of the Holocaust felt.

Controversy

But Eisenman's memorial caused **controversy** (disagreement). Some people felt it needed more facts to educate people about the Holocaust. The German government later added a visitor center with educational materials.

Eisenman's Berlin Holocaust Memorial opened in 2005.

Design a September 11 memorial

There has been a lot of **debate** (discussion) about what sort of memorial is best to remember the victims of the September 11, 2001, terrorist attacks in New York City and the Pentagon. There have been different ideas for a memorial on the site where the World Trade Center's Twin Towers once stood in New York.

Steps to follow:

1. Begin by sketching out your ideas with a pencil and paper. Will there be sculptures or fountains? Will you include the names of the victims? Will you build on the site where the Twin Towers once stood, or leave that empty?

2. Bring your sketch to life as a **diorama**. Find a shoebox or cardboard box and place this on its side. You can use clay, cardboard, or construction paper to make buildings, statues, or fountains.

3. Begin by painting or drawing a background in the back of the box. Then create the different pieces of your memorial and glue them in place, moving from back to front.

4. Ask a group of friends or family to come view your memorial. Do they agree with your choices?

A diorama will allow you to explore ideas about memorials.

The actual memorial in New York City is a park with two square pools of water standing where the Twin Towers once stood. The names of the victims are carved on structures surrounding the pools. A museum is also on the site. How does this compare to your ideas for your own memorial?

Political Public Art

Since ancient times, public art has been used for **political** purposes. This takes on many forms.

Obelisks

Obelisks are often placed in city centers to symbolize a leader's power. An obelisk is a tall structure, usually made of stone, that has four sides and often a point on top.

The Black Obelisk of Shalmaneser III was made in what is now northern Iraq. The Assyrian government **commissioned** this work when Shalmaneser III ruled, from 858 to 824 BCE. The obelisk's carvings show events from Shalmaneser's life, such as military victories and gifts he received. It served as a record of his power and importance.

The Black Obelisk of Shalmaneser III is now in London's British Museum.

The Arch of Constantine (315 CE) still stands in Rome.

Triumphal arches

The ancient Roman government commissioned the Arch of Constantine (315 CE) to honor an important military victory by Constantine I. It also honored his first ten years as emperor. This work is a **triumphal arch**.

The arch's carvings show Constantine's victories. It also shows past Roman leaders, connecting Constantine with Rome's history. The arch was built on an important parade path. The Roman army followed this path, surrounded by cheering crowds, after military victories.

The work's style and location encouraged the Roman people to connect Constantine with power and victory. It also made them feel **patriotic** (proud of their country).

More obelisks and columns

Another important obelisk is the Washington **Monument** (1884) in Washington, D.C., honoring President George Washington. **Columns** are similar to obelisks, but they are round, rather than having four sides. Nelson's Column (1843), in London's Trafalgar Square, honors Admiral Horatio Nelson, a British war hero.

Political portraits

Political leaders have always understood the power of portraits. Mao Zedong was a Chinese leader who came to power in 1949. He became a **totalitarian** ruler, meaning he had total control over people's lives.

Mao commissioned enormous sculptures of himself that appeared in most public squares. In works like the one at left, he is shown as **heroic** and larger than life.

These sculptures made some people feel patriotic. But these enormous works could also cause fear in Chinese citizens who questioned Mao's total power.

If you were a Chinese citizen how would this statue of Mao Zedong make you feel about your leader?

Rejecting political art

When a leader starts to lose power, people often respond by tearing down public art showing that leader. For example, when Soviet leader Josef Stalin fell out of favor beginning in the 1960s, monuments made for him were destroyed—often with dynamite, because the monuments were so enormous!

Dedicate a work of political art

When a major work of political art is created, there is often a **dedication** ceremony. This means that the work is officially revealed to the public. Important people give speeches about the work.

In this activity, you will play the role of an artist who has honored a political leader with a triumphal arch. You will give a speech at a dedication ceremony.

Steps to follow:

1. Choose a leader to honor.

2. Decide how to build your arch. You could use blocks or cardboard boxes. You could also draw on sheets of paper and tape them to a wall.

3. Write a speech explaining how the work presents the leader. For example, does it show how brave and strong he or she is?

4. Gather a group of friends to help you act out the dedication ceremony. Some will play everyday people, some could be military leaders, and someone could be the leader.

5. Give your speech.

Try covering your triumphal arch with drawings of historical scenes.

Religious Public Art

Since the beginning of history, religious groups have built public art. Religions from around the world create art to inspire believers.

Buddhism

Buddhism is an ancient Asian religion. Buddhists honor a man named Siddhartha Gautama, also known as the Buddha. They believe he achieved a state of perfect enlightenment, a way of living that escapes suffering.

Fenxian Cave

Fengxian Cave houses the largest Buddha statue at the Longmen Caves. It stands at over 57 feet (17 meters) tall.

Longmen Caves

In the 400s CE, a place called Luoyang was used as a **political** center in China. A series of **devout** (very religious) Chinese rulers wanted a public place of worship nearby. They **commissioned** the construction of the Longmen Caves, a series of 1,342 caves built along two mountains. The caves feature more than 100,000 statues (see box above) and countless carvings that show Buddhist images and symbols.

The number of works and beauty of the Longmen Caves inspire **awe** (wonder) in many visitors.

This is a dramatic entry to Angkor Wat.

Hinduism

Hinduism is another long-standing Asian religion. Hindus believe that people struggle to break free from a cycle of reincarnation, or rebirth. They hope to lead their lives in such a way that they will break from this cycle. Hindus worship many gods.

Angkor Wat

In the 1100s, in present-day Cambodia, a devout Hindu leader named Suryavarman II commissioned a series of temples.

Angkor Wat is the most well-known of these temples. Covering 500 acres (200 hectares) of land, it is a huge structure decorated with thousands of sculptures and stone carvings of Buddhist and Hindu images and symbols, especially the god Vishnu. Visitors to this public art site are often overwhelmed by the experience.

Christianity

Christianity has a long history in Europe. This religion later spread to other parts of the world, including North America and Latin America.

Christians believe that God's son, Jesus Christ, suffered and died for people's sins. God, Jesus Christ, and the Holy Spirit are all part of one God whom most Christians worship.

The enormous statue shows Christ with open arms, seeming to embrace all of Rio. It is positioned on the top of Corcovado Mountain, which overlooks the city. In this way, the statue serves as a constant reminder of Christ to Rio's citizens as they go about their everyday lives.

The Renaissance

The **Renaissance** was a period from roughly 1400 to 1600, when talented artists created masterworks of art throughout Europe. The Roman Catholic Church often commissioned this artwork. Public churches became filled with beautiful examples of stained glass, paintings, and sculpture for the public to experience, such as Michelangelo's *Pietà* (c. 1499), in St. Peter's Basilica, in Rome.

Michelangelo's *Pietà* (c. 1499) shows the Virgin Mary (Jesus Christ's mother) cradling the dead body of Christ.

The statue stands at 130 feet (39.6 meters) tall. That is as tall as a 13-story building! The statue's overwhelming size inspires awe in all who see it.

A towering Christ

Christianity is very strong in Brazil. In the 1920s, a group of Brazilian Catholics raised money to build a statue of Jesus Christ in Rio de Janeiro. They wanted a symbol of Christ in the center of their city. Sculpted by Frenchman Paul Landowski, *Christ the Redeemer* was completed in 1931.

Visitors climb to Landowski's *Christ the Redeemer* (1931) and see amazing views of Rio.

Public Sculpture

Sometimes public art is made simply to provide an experience of art in everyday life.

Abstract sculpture

In Western cultures, in the late 1960s, many cities and companies **commissioned** large works of public sculpture. These were meant to educate people about modern art and make cities beautiful. Important **abstract** artists, such as Pablo Picasso, Henry Moore, and Isamu Noguchi, created public art in many cities.

Tilted Arc

In 1981 U.S. artist Richard Serra revealed *Tilted Arc*, a curving wall of steel. It was positioned in a **plaza** (open area) surrounded by government buildings in New York City.

Serra's *Tilted Arc* (1981) was 120 feet (37 meters) long.

The art world admired the bold work. But many government workers felt it was too enormous and dark. It also made it difficult to move through the plaza. Workers complained, and a judge ruled that *Tilted Arc* should be taken down.

Remembering the public

After this **controversy**, artists often thought more about the public. For example, U.S. artist Jeff Koons's giant *Puppy* (see cover) makes many viewers smile.

British artist Antony Gormley's *Angel of the North* (1998), in Gateshead, England, speaks to local people. It was built where coal mines once stood. Gormley wanted the work to remind people of this history and to represent hope for the future. Many people see the figure as a guardian angel watching over their region.

Taxes

Titled Arc was part of a government program. This means everyday people paid for it with **taxes**. Should people have a say in public art paid for with their tax money?

Gormley's *Angel of the North* (1998), located by a major highway, is seen by many people.

19

Other Forms of Public Art

Public art is not always **monuments** and sculpture. **Murals**, posters, **graffiti**, and street performers are additional forms of public art.

Murals

A mural is a large work of art painted on a wall or ceiling. Murals are often painted on public property, for all to see.

Mexican murals

Murals have a long history in Mexico. In the 1920s, a new Mexican government wanted to support and respect everyday people—a change from the last government's ideas. This new government wanted to communicate these goals to the people.

However, much of the public could not read. So the government **commissioned** artists to paint murals on public buildings throughout the country. These murals would be a new way to communicate.

A popular art form

Murals are not only made by famous artists. They are also an easy way for local groups to create a work of public art. Murals create a sense of community.

Muralists with a purpose

The three greatest Mexican muralists were Diego Rivera, José Clemente Orozco, and David Alfaro Siqueiros. All three artists believed that art's purpose is to educate people. In their murals they painted scenes from Mexico's history, alongside images showing a strong future for Mexico.

This is a detail from Rivera's final public mural, made in 1953 at the Mexican Institute of Social Security. It shows how Mexicans could look forward to better health care.

Beginning in the 1920s, Rivera painted murals in the halls and on the outside walls of government buildings throughout Mexico. Some murals focus on the hard work of everyday people, who are shown as **heroic**. Others focus on the people's festivals and artwork. Everyday people would see these murals and feel respected. They would feel—as the government wanted them to feel—that they played a central role in Mexico's future.

Posters

Posters are another form of public art. They are displayed in public places such as subways or busy city streets. Posters are often used to sell products. They can also be **political**.

During the 2008 United States presidential election, artist Shepard Fairey created a poster using a news photograph of Barack Obama, the colors of the U.S. flag, and the word *hope*. This presented Obama as a strong, heroic leader. Supporters displayed hundreds of thousands of copies of this poster across the United States.

Street performances

Sometimes street performances, such as those by musicians, break dancers, or mimes, are classified as "public art."

Graffiti

Graffiti is art created on someone else's property, such as the subway. Some graffiti is beautiful or clever, while other work is not skillful. The problem with graffiti is that the property owner must give permission. Otherwise, making graffiti is against the law.

Graffiti is illegal unless you have permission from the property owner.

Create a sound sculpture

In this project, you will create a sound sculpture by attaching objects that make sound to a clay sculpture.

Steps to follow:

1. Think about what sort of sculpture you will make. It could represent an object (such as a bird) or be **abstract** (see page 18).

2. Model the shape of your sculpture with clay. You could paint it, too.

3. Choose materials that will create a chiming sound when they move in the wind—for example, silverware, keys, or metal tubes. Delicate chimes may sound more like a bird in flight than heavy crashing noises.

4. Experiment with ways to attach these musical parts to your sculpture, probably with string or fishing line.

5. Place your sculpture somewhere outside where the wind will be able to move the chimes and produce sound, such as a tree branch.

6. Invite friends or family to come look at and listen to your work of public art.

How does sound change the experience of public art?

How do your friends and family respond to your sound sculpture?

Public Art in Nature

Public art can also be a part of nature. Things such as rocks, water, and flowers can be used to create public art.

Robert Smithson

Earth art is a movement that started in the 1960s, when more people began to care more about the environment. These artists use nature for their materials.

In 1970 U.S. artist Robert Smithson created *Spiral Jetty* in the Great Salt Lake, in Utah. An art gallery gave him the money to do this. Smithson used rocks and earth from the site to create a huge coil in the dramatic red water. When water levels are right, visitors can walk on the coil.

The work makes people see nature as a kind of art. It also makes people travel to visit public art.

Smithson's *Spiral Jetty* (1970) is 1,500 feet (460 meters) long.

People walking the *Chalk Stones Trail* find 15 chalk stones throughout the 5-mile (8-kilometer) walk.

Andy Goldsworthy

In 2002 British artist Andy Goldsworthy was **commissioned** by government groups to make the *Chalk Stones Trail* in West Sussex, England. He formed 14 large chalkstones and placed them throughout the landscape. The idea was for people to find all the stones—a 5-mile (8-kilometer) nature walk!

Goldsworthy encouraged people to experience nature. By using chalk native to West Sussex, he also created public art that connects to the area's history.

Ikebana

In Japan *ikebana*, the art of flower arrangement, is a long-standing art form. Usually these flower arrangements are shown in indoor spaces.

In recent years, however, a popular public *ikebana* show has been held on a fashionable street in Tokyo, Japan. Flower displays line the streets and bring beauty and nature to everyday life—which is important in a crowded city like Tokyo.

The Future of Public Art

Recent works of public art have moved toward being **ephemeral**. This means that they are not meant to last.

The Gates

In 2005 Bulgarian-born U.S. artist Christo and French-born U.S. artist Jean-Claude created *The Gates*. They installed 7,500 gates hung with orange fabric in New York City's Central Park. The project was taken down after two weeks.

Some New Yorkers loved the gates and felt they added fun and beauty to city life. But others thought the gates made it difficult to move through the park, or they simply didn't like the look of them.

Christo and Jean-Claude paid for *The Gates* (2005) themselves. Does this give them more freedom to do as they like?

The fourth plinth

London's Trafalgar Square is a busy central place. Its "fourth **plinth**" is an empty base made to hold a **memorial** statue that was never built. Beginning in 1999, government groups **commissioned** artists to temporarily fill this plinth.

In 2009 British artist Antony Gormley used the fourth plinth for his *One & Other* project. For 100 days he invited people to take turns standing on the plinth for an hour at a time and do whatever they wished.

Some people argued this was great public art because it directly involved the public. But other people didn't think this project was "art." What do you think?

In Gormley's *One & Other* (2009), people themselves became the artwork.

What next?

There will always be **debates** like this about what public art should be. People care deeply about public art, because it is the art of our everyday lives.

Timeline

C. 825 BCE	Black **Obelisk** of Shalmaneser III is completed in ancient Assyria.
315 CE	Arch of Constantine is completed in ancient Rome.
400s	The carving of the Longmen Caves are completed near Luoyang, China.
1100s	Construction begins on Angkor Wat, in present-day Cambodia.
c. 1499	Italian artist Michelangelo completes his *Pietà* in Rome.
1843	British **architect** William Railton's Nelson's **Column** is completed in London, England.
1876	British architect Sir George Gilbert Scott's Albert **Memorial** is completed in London.
1884	U.S. architect Robert Mills's Washington **Monument** is completed in Washington, D.C.
1922	U.S. architect Henry Bacon's and U.S. sculptor Daniel Chester French's Lincoln Memorial is completed in Washington, D.C.
1920s	Mexican artist Diego Rivera begins creating public **murals** throughout Mexico.
1931	French sculptor Paul Landowski's *Christ the Redeemer* is completed in Rio de Janeiro, Brazil.
1960s	Large works of public sculpture are **commissioned** by governments and companies throughout the Western world.
1970	U.S. artist Robert Smithson's *Spiral Jetty* is completed in the Great Salt Lake, Utah.

1981	U.S. artist Richard Serra's *Tilted Arc* is completed in New York City. It is taken down in 1989.
1982	U.S. architect Maya Lin's Vietnam Veterans Memorial is completed in Washington, D.C.
1992	U.S. artist Jeff Koons's *Puppy* is completed. In 1997 it is moved to Bilbao, Spain.
1992	Statue of Mao Zedong is erected in Lijiang, Yunnan, China.
1998	British artist Antony Gormley's *Angel of the North* is completed in Gateshead, England.
2000s	*Ikebana* flower shows become a popular outdoor public art form in Tokyo, Japan.
2002	British artist Andy Goldsworthy's *Chalk Stones Trail* is completed in West Sussex, England.
2005	U.S. architect Peter Eisenman's Holocaust Memorial is opened in Berlin, Germany.
2005	Bulgarian-born U.S. artist Christo's and French-born U.S. artist Jeanne-Claude's *Gates* are completed in New York City's Central Park.
2008	U.S. artist Shepard Fairey completes his "Hope" poster of Barack Obama.
2009	British artist Antony Gormley's *One & Other* project is held in London's Trafalgar Square.

Glossary

abstract not realistic

architect person who designs buildings

awe sense of wonder

column tall structure, usually made of stone, that is rounded. Columns are often monuments to important leaders.

commission ask an artist to make something that you will pay for

controversy disagreement

debate discussion

dedication ceremony in which a building or work of art is revealed to the public, often with speeches about the work

devout very religious

Earth art style of art that began in the 1960s. Artists use materials from nature and focus on the environment.

ephemeral not permanent or lasting

graffiti art created on someone else's property

heroic brave; like a hero

ikebana Japanese art of flower arranging

memorial work of art that is put in a public place to honor the lives of others or to cause viewers to reflect on tragedies; also called a monument

monument large work of art that is placed in a public place to remember a person or event; also called a memorial

mural large work of art painted on a wall or ceiling

obelisk tall structure, usually made of stone, that has four sides and often ends with a point on top. Obelisks are often monuments to important leaders.

patriotic proud of one's country

plaza open area near public buildings

plinth base for a statue or monument

political related to governments

reflect think closely about something

Renaissance period in Europe from about 1400 to 1600, when many great works of art were created and new ideas were explored

tax money that people are required to pay to their government

totalitarian government that has total power over its people

triumphal arch arch built to honor a leader or victory

Find Out More

Books

d'Harcourt, Claire. *Art Up Close: From Ancient to Modern*. San Francisco: Chronicle, 2006.

Renshaw, Amanda, and Gilda Williams Ruggi. *The Art Book for Children*. New York: Phaidon, 2005.

Spilsbury, Richard. *Stories in Art: Sculpture*. New York: PowerKids, 2008.

Organizations to contact

The following organizations are dedicated to art and public art. There might be local groups dedicated to supporting public art in your community. Do research to find the groups nearest you.

National Endowment for the Arts
1100 Pennsylvania Avenue, NW
Washington DC 20506
www.nea.gov

Americans for the Arts
1000 Vermont Avenue, NW
6th Floor
Washington DC 20005
www.artsusa.org/networks/public_art_network

Index